Testimonials

"Larry Baker touches on a very stigmatized and poorly understood topic of suicide in a refreshing and compassionate way. His life is an example of the highest of highs, lowest of lows and how we as a human race carry a lot of karma into these bodies of ours. Society pressures, religion and expectations to "succeed" in a material world, can lead us to madness. It can happen to ANYONE. It all begins with a shift in consciousness, and I loved his analogy of going into another room of the mind. He normalizes suicide in a way that isn't crass or disrespectful. THAT is what the world needs to hear/see/learn from. Having lost thirteen people that I loved to suicide and even more to addiction, finding myself pondering this decision, I totally get it and am grateful to Larry for sharing his story and wisdom. So many deserve to read this—those who are considering suicide, those who have lost a loved one and, yes, even those who may judge this choice."

—Magdalena Grace, Suicide awareness podcaster and advocate

"Crisp. Tight. The story draws me in. It's captivating. I never had a desire to end my life, but through this story, I have gained a great deal of compassion and understanding."

—Lorraine Seeley Buell, author of *Shipmates, A Personal Journal Aboard a WW II Destroyer*

"In this very honest book, Larry tackles the profound questions of one's fate and its meaning. A rare read."

—Hajime Ohno, fellow Fallbrook Artist

"From the very first words in the introduction, Larry Baker's *Suicide Survivor* is a gripping, heartfelt journey through the pain of mental disorientation, often endured by those who have thoughts of suicide. Of primal importance, the book is about hope and how to achieve a worthwhile and fulfilling life.The book reaches inside one to the most basic of human dilemmas: shall I live or die?. The author's experience was life-changing and affirming for him, and it can be for the individual reader as well—especially if that reader, or someone they know, is having thoughts of suicide. Baker points out the futility of suicide and reminds us "there's a lot you don't know about the rest of your life". The book asserts the worth of every human being and the good that can come from interacting, helping and reaching out to others. I found this memoir to be thought provoking—and hopefully, life preserving. Well worth the time it takes to consider what is presented."

—Sean Mark Witan, MBA

"*Suicide Survivor* is a deeply personal and reflective memoir that delves into the author's near-death experience with suicide and his journey toward healing and self-discovery. The book is structured to provide both a narrative of Baker's life and practical advice for those struggling with suicidal thoughts. Through vivid storytelling, Baker recounts his time in Vietnam, his struggles with mental health, and the pivotal moments that led him to choose life over self-destruction. The book's strength lies in its raw honesty and the author's willingness to share his vulnerabilities, making it relatable and impactful for readers who may be facing similar challenges. The inclusion of resources, practical tips, and reflections on spirituality adds depth and utility to the narrative, offering readers a comprehensive guide to navigating their own struggles.

Suicide Survivor is a heartfelt and courageous work that has the potential to inspire and provide solace to those in crisis. Its central message—that life is worth living and that there is always hope—shines through, making it a valuable resource for individuals seeking understanding and support."

—Jack Kovic, Former Editor Naval Hospital, Camp Pendleton Public Affairs Office

Suicide Survivor

By Larry Baker

Suicide Survivor

Published in the United States of America by Larry Baker

Identifiers:
979-8-9996000-0-4 (Paperback)
979-8-9996000-1-1 (Ebook)

URGENT

IF YOU OR SOMEONE YOU KNOW ARE HAVING THOUGHTS OF SUICIDE OR ARE IN EXTREME EMOTIONAL DISTRESS, CALL THE SUICIDE PREVENTION HOTLINE AT 988 OR (800) 273-8255 (TALK).

IF YOU OR SOMEONE YOU KNOW ARE THE VICTIM OF ABUSE, CALL 911 FOR IMMEDIATE ASSISTANCE. IN THE US, CALL THE NATIONAL DOMESTIC VIOLENCE HOTLINE AT (800) 799-7233 (SAFE) OR SEARCH WOMENSLAW.ORG'S STATE-BY-STATE DIRECTORY OF DOMESTIC VIOLENCE SHELTERS AND ADVOCATES.

DISCLAIMER

THE AUTHOR IS NOT A PSYCHOLOGIST, PSYCHOTHERAPIST NOR A MEDICAL DOCTOR. THUS, HE CANNOT PRESCRIBE MEDICINES, THERAPIES OR CURES. ANY ADVICE OR SUGGESTIONS REGARDING SUICIDE PREVENTION ARE SOLELY BASED ON HIS OWN EXPERIENCE OR THOSE OF THE OTHER AUTHORS QUOTED HEREIN.

Table of Contents

PART III: YOUR SPIRITUAL LIFE

"I pick up the weapon with cool detachment. My world has shrunk to this small cubicle I will never walk out of alive again.

"I turn the rifle around and place the cold steel barrel against the bridge of my nose, right between my eyes. Only seconds away now, I am committed. I am going to do it . . . all alone in the dead of night. I can almost feel the bullet slamming into my frontal lobe, exploding my brains.

"Looking around calmly, keenly observing, I feel my blood pulsing for the last time.

"I close my eyes . . . I am ready now. Gently putting the slightest touch on the trigger, flesh on steel . . . a few ounces more pressure and there will be a pop and a jerk and I will be gone . . ."

Suicide Survivor

A Year in the War

Introduction

Hello, I'm Larry Baker—a Suicide Survivor. What is that? It's a person—maybe someone like you or someone you love—who has come very close to suicide, but who, for one reason or another, has *survived.* You have lived to tell about it. Maybe you overdosed on drugs and would have died, but someone found you and called 911. Emergency medical staff arrived in time to save your life.

Maybe you were thinking about it, but called the Suicide Prevention Hotline, 800-273-TALK, and were guided toward some life-saving counseling. Maybe you experienced what some call "divine intervention"—like I believe I did—and were saved at the last crucial moment.

What is your situation? Have you already survived a suicide attempt or have things gotten so bad you're considering it? Either way, this book is for you—even if you are not pondering suicide.

You may know someone who is. I'm hoping my story will help others recognize the conditions that are setting him or her on a path toward oblivion.

In my case, I came within a *moment* of suicide: self-destruction, early termination, kicking the bucket or whatever else you want to call the act of ending one's own life.

However, if you *have* been thinking about suicide, but somehow you found this book, then you have a chance—a real opportunity—to delay it and possibly postpone it forever. Why? Because I did. What I learned from my experience has taught me that there is a lot we don't know about the rest of our lives! Joys and sorrows. Good times and bad. It's all a journey that, no matter the darkness of the present moment, is worth the effort. You are worth the effort. You are worthy of the gift of your life. You are a unique and valuable being. The best is yet to come!

If you don't believe me, I get it. I've been there, too. I appreciate your skepticism. That's healthy, but what if there is something beyond these feelings you have: the sadness, emptiness and loneliness? I invite you to come along with me on my path of self-discovery—from that pivotal moment to where I am today. Maybe there is something in my experience that can help you. That is my fondest hope.

Suicide is one of those topics that people don't want to talk about. It's got such a stigma attached to it: "Only a coward would do such a thing." "You're taking the easy way out." "It's the unforgivable sin." If those voices are in your head right now, tell them to take a vacation while you view the path of self-destruction from another, higher point of view.

The first question on everyone's mind is, "Why do people choose suicide in the first place?" I'm not a psychologist, so I'm going to avoid the technical terms, but most experts say the simple answer is depression. It's the umbrella that overshadows many suicidal thoughts and feelings, such as loneliness, pain, rejection, or sadness. The dictionary says depression is "a condition of general emotional dejection and withdrawal, sadness greater and more prolonged than that warranted by any objective reason." It has been said that depression is cancer of the soul. The pain can be physical, emotional, psychological or a combination of all three, but it is so intense that the person in pain eventually, after all other remedies fail, considers suicide. In my case, it felt like there was no way out. I was in over my head and drowning in my delusions with no one to save me. It was a waking nightmare.

There are probably many things people aren't aware of which explain how they get to a place in life where they want to end it all. (If there even is such a thing as ending it all. We'll get to that later.)

As we delve into the cause, effects, and solutions to the despair where you may find yourself, I'll show you how I found my way out of the darkness. I discovered other options. In the Bible, John 14:2, Christ says, "In my Father's house are many mansions." Suicide is just one of the rooms in the mansion of your mind. Some call it a *state of consciousness*, which you can change at any moment, as I will explain. Leave one room and enter another. It might take a little practice, but after a while, it gets easier. It can be as easy as switching a channel on TV.

I'm inviting you to read my story of how I came within a few seconds of suicide but was miraculously saved at the last moment. I'd like you to know what I went through and how my life turned around after what I call a miraculous, divine intervention.

Along with my story, be sure to review the resources in the Appendix at the end. This will give you a better understanding of what your options are. And remember: "There's a lot you don't know about the rest of your life!"

PART I

CHAPTER 1

A Year in the War

Suicide? No one would have *ever* thought I was a candidate. Eerily, a strange turn of events catapulted me from sanity into paranoid schizophrenia. How could an intelligent, well-educated, healthy, young man from a loving family—a former altar boy and devout Catholic—end up a moment away from suicide?

As strange as it may seem, it all had to do with religion. Yes, I was in the war-torn country of Vietnam. There was the daily stress of being stationed at an Assault Helicopter Base. When I walked through the local town of Soc Trang, outside our army compound, some of the locals were friendly, smiling, with cheerful looks that conveyed, "Glad you are here in our country protecting us and our freedom" but others were unfriendly, condescending, cold stares which read as, “What are you doing in my country and how soon can you leave? You are not welcome here. We will solve our own problems internally without intervention by you and the US Army.” True, I was not out fighting in the jungle with the infantry, but one had to be careful every minute of each day. The enemy was always nearby, sometimes passing you on the street in town—the ones who didn’t smile.

A tour of duty in Vietnam, however, brought many possibilities. It reminded me of the opening lines of Charles Dickens’ masterpiece, *A Tale of Two Cities*: “It was the best of times. It was the worst of times.” For starters, I was finally free. I had just turned 21, so I was legally an adult, but more importantly, I was free of parental control. Yes, my father drilled into me the importance of getting a college degree, but I had bombed out of college twice. In those days, if you didn’t have a college deferment, and in good standing with your school, you were certain to be drafted into the army.

That is exactly what happened. College was tough for me. I didn’t have much money and had to commute daily to and from Cal State L.A.—a campus of 32,000 students—in an old 1949 Chevy. In contrast, my Catholic all boys’ high school had only 350 students, taught by very strict Dominican Brothers who ran a tight ship. Any boys late for class or without their homework would be sent to detention after school for a few strokes of the strap.

I was overwhelmed. In college I had too much freedom. Plus, there was a constant parade of beautiful young women to distract me from my studies. And I wasn’t sure what I wanted for a career. My brother Bob was two years ahead of me and had already decided on engineering as his major. I was focused on business, so I chose real estate classes. It was hard. I was not a good student and my grades suffered. Along the way, I fell in love with one of my classmates. However, her father was a staunch Baptist. Since I was a Catholic, he forbade us to continue dating. Soon, my high school friend, Gil, and I started playing cards in the morning at the college cafeteria. At noon, the campus gym opened, and we would spend a few hours playing basketball. At the end of that school year, I was notified that I would not be allowed to return because of my low grade-point average. I got a job with the railroad, but within a few months I was drafted into the US Army and on a bus heading to my basic training at Fort Ord in Monterey, California. After ten weeks of basic training on the coast, I was sent to Fort Gordon, Georgia, for advanced training as a teletype operator. At the conclusion of training, I received my orders for deployment to Vietnam.

When we landed at the airport in Saigon, I was certain the Vietcong—the enemy—would be shooting at us as we deplaned. Surprisingly, it was tranquil, peaceful and calm as I walked down the ramp. Little did I know that the greatest danger facing me in Vietnam would be myself!

My initial assignment was with the 52nd Signal Battalion in a mid-size city called Can Tho. We lived in an old four-story French villa converted to an army barracks with ten soldiers per apartment, most of them from California. We worked hard during the days, manning our communication hutches or filling sandbags during off hours. At night we partied hard—every night. There were plenty of local bars with pretty girls wanting us to buy them drinks, but we often went back to our barracks where the beer and hard liquor were inexpensive, purchased from our PX. We could play loud music and drink until we passed out. By now I was smoking two packs of menthol cigarettes a day and drinking heavily. One night I fell asleep smoking a cigarette and my mattress caught fire. From the third floor, my roommates threw my bedding over the balcony. They found another mattress to replace mine from another room where someone was out on guard duty. Hung-over the next morning, I had no memory of the event. I don't count that as a Near Death Experience, but it certainly could have been. It was just another one of my poor decisions, which could have been fatal.

• • •

After six months in Can Tho, and with too much carousing around town under the influence of alcohol and copious amounts of Vietnamese marijuana, Sergeant Miller decided I needed a change. I was reassigned to a smaller town, Soc Trang, also in the Mekong River Delta. My new job was on the night shift babysitting the Air Force operator of the weather machine. If it had any problems, I was to call the army repairman, who was down in the barracks asleep, and ensure he arose and came up to the tower to repair the machine. Apparently, when the repairman was called in the past, he would promise to "be right there" but then turn over and go back to sleep. My job was to go get him and physically escort him up to the tower. A meaningless, unnecessary job created by some general tired of hearing all the complaints.

I soon struck up a series of conversations with one of the air traffic controllers, a man named Sean Murphy. He was a private contractor with the status of Major who had previously served in the US Air Force for four years where he learned the craft of air traffic control. Since we were stationed at an assault helicopter base, it could get very busy during the days, but on the night shift we had a chance to get acquainted.

Growing up in Belfast, Northern Ireland, he was a Catholic, as I was, but had left the church years ago. We spent hours discussing what was right or wrong with the church. While I had led a fairly sheltered life, Sean was eight years my senior and had traveled all over Europe during his Air Force deployment in Ramstein Air Base in Germany. We became friends and began to spend time together during our off hours as well as our work shifts, whenever they coincided.

During one of our lengthy philosophical discussions, he explained that he was no longer a Catholic. I asked why. "For one thing," he said, "there are over eight million Buddhists here in Vietnam. According to the tenets of Catholicism, they will all go to hell!"

We went back and forth about the Catholic Church because at that point in my life—even though I had taken to drink and drugs—I still considered myself a Catholic.

His reply was simply, "Well, maybe that's your *karma*."

I froze in place, as if I had been shot with a bolt of lightning. "Wait," I said. "What's that word you just said?"

"Karma," he replied, surprised that I hadn't heard of it. "Very simply, it's known as the spiritual Law of Returns: Cause and Effect. It's mentioned in the Bible: "As ye sow, so shall ye reap." In simple terms, whatever energy you put out into the world is going to come back to you in one form or another, either in this life or the next. It's a spiritual boomerang."

I was spellbound, absorbing every word as if I were waking from a dream and hearing truth for the first time. He wove in the theory of reincarnation, the other part of this ancient twin doctrine which explains every part of our lives, our history, our goals, likes and dislikes, as well as how we can eventually graduate from Planet Earth—and from the need to ever reincarnate again.

Mesmerized, I wanted to know more, to learn all about it. He finally held up his hands in protest. "Look," he said, "if you are really interested, I will loan you a book about all this stuff—but only on one condition. You only get the book for one week. If you haven't read it by then, you promise to give it back to me."

I agreed, eager to get my hands on the book, which he had for me the next day. I devoured that initial book in a few days. It was about a Tibetan Lama named Lobsang Rampa. Nine more books followed over the next few weeks with many discussions during our night shifts in the control tower. These books painted a completely different version of reality compared with how I had been brainwashed by the doctrines of 1960s Catholicism.

Lobsang, the author, recounted his upbringing in the Potala, the famous Tibetan Monastery in the Himalayas—the towering mountains of Northern Tibet. Lobsang recalled his early childhood, where he was forced to leave his family and enter the lamasery for training as a monk. He was surrounded by similar boys who had also been chosen, plucked from homes in the villages below to enter the austere life to be trained as lamas. The daily routine was intense, and the teachers, themselves lamas, were strict.

Lobsang, however, had a unique skill. From an early age, he was able to travel out of his body at night and explore the dream worlds, which he termed the astral realm. His body for these travels and schooling was similar to his earthly, physical form—still asleep on his cot at the lamasery—but of a higher rate of vibration, allowing him to travel at the speed of thought. At night in the astral regions, he attended classes, visited museums and enjoyed a wide variety of experiences that would both prepare him and benefit him later in life.

In the books, Lobsang taught that each of us, as spiritual beings, return to earth many times, to both pay off our karma and also transcend the reach of the five passions of the mind—greed, anger, lust, vanity and attachment—on our way to spiritual liberation. Self-realization would lead to God consciousness. And it was all based on God's love for each of us.

While reincarnation is an ongoing educational system, karma provides a way for each soul to atone for any wrongdoings or missteps along the way. But it wasn't just about punishment. Positive actions or efforts in past lives would find their way as rewards in the future. This twin doctrine provided an all-inclusive package, which explained anything that could happen to anyone, anywhere—past, present or future—along the journey of his or her lives. One of the key goals of life was to learn how to love and be loved in return.

After reading these ten books, I let go of Christianity because it didn't include all of humanity as possible candidates for heaven. I still loved Jesus, but I wanted something that welcomed *everyone* and reasoned that if God was smart enough to create all of us, IT (not He) ought to be wise enough to figure out a way whereby we could all eventually reach heaven. The efficient part about reincarnation is that it gives everyone an unlimited number of lives to achieve liberation, or freedom from rebirth. Karma was simply a universal justice system that allowed everyone a way to right their wrongs, learn their lessons and master the spiritual laws of the universe. Then the fun began.

• • •

Soon after, Sean was reassigned to another city. This was unfortunate for me, as he might have been able to offset some of the delusions I was gradually developing about who I had been in past lives. And I might have been able to navigate the metaphysical minefield better than I did.

But he was gone. I felt alone, abandoned, and unable to share my new wisdom with anyone. I was different from everyone around me because they didn't know how the world really worked. I did . . . or so I thought.

Soon, I fell in with some of the guys from my barracks. We started going to the Enlisted Men's Club on base, or after work for fun downtown. One fateful night began with two of us sharing a bottle of Jack Daniels, and ended with a drunken brawl outside the Club. I was knocked unconscious. When other soldiers found me later and turned me over, my face was a bloody mess.

I awoke the next morning in the compound hospital to a blinding white light bursting in from the midmorning sun. When I rubbed my eyes open, I became aware the entire room was bathed in white: white floors, white walls, white ceiling and nurses dressed in white. For a moment, I felt like I had died and gone to heaven. The head-splitting pain of my hangover, coupled with the swelling in my head and face from the punches I received during the previous night, brought me back to reality.

The doctor came in and told me he had taken a total of fifty-seven stiches on various parts of my face, but that I should be okay—and to lay off the booze for a while. Good luck with that! I was released later that afternoon.

• • •

What complicated matters was that, like many new converts to karma and reincarnation, I began to have *delusions of grandeur* about who I might have been in a past life. Inflated egos cause many to believe they must have been a king or a queen or Elvis or Marilyn Monroe. I read meaning into *everything.* Numbers and letters had special significance, implications or hidden clues. I viewed everyone I knew as some memorable personage from history.

My bloated ego convinced me that I had obviously been incarnated as an archetype for humanity, possibly another world savior, or maybe another Christ-like being.

I was certainly an important soul to have such a panoramic viewpoint—that I must be on a *special mission* of massive importance. Like Christ, or the Tibetan Lama Lobsang Rampa, I would do something great. Maybe I was Christ . . . *reincarnated*?

I looked in the mirror one morning and saw the triangular shape my eyes made with the forehead scar from the beating outside the EM Club. The significance of this was suddenly clear—the Catholic trinity: God, the Holy Spirit, and Jesus. It was now obvious to me that I was the reincarnation of *Jesus*!

Ecstatic, I was overjoyed! However, the Jesus persona was not without a dark side. A persecution complex subtly snaked its way into my consciousness. I felt attacked from all sides. The thick layer of normal psychological protection disintegrated. Acutely sensitive to the hidden meanings of the most inconsequential comments I might overhear, I wore the savior complex—a belief that I had once been Jesus—with alcohol and drug-induced delusion, a recipe for disaster.

• • •

The savior complex soon took a 180-degree turn. Whatever connection I thought I had to a former incarnation as Jesus evaporated. A fate far worse awaited me.

There is a humorous saying attributed to Yogi Berra of New York Yankees fame: "If you come to a fork in the road, take it!" Obviously, with a fork in the road, one must either turn to the left or the right. My fork in the road went like this: On one of my travels for medical treatment, I came across another soldier who, I noticed, had a scar in the middle of his forehead. He was very cheerful, happy and outgoing. Sitting across from him in the waiting room, I was stunned. For one thing, he was black! I quickly reconfigured my thinking. First, there couldn't be two persons reincarnating as Jesus. Also, if Jesus were going to come back to earth, he probably wouldn't return as a Caucasian. It would be more fitting and appropriate for him to return as another highly persecuted race, such as an Afro-American. Remember, this was 1967, when the USA was still is the midst of extreme racial persecution.

Something shifted, as if the floor fell away. Kicking into high gear, my persecution paranoia veered off on a terrifying tangent. Whatever the logic or reasoning, the picture now painfully clear to me was that this cheerful black soldier *must* be the reincarnation of Jesus. If that was the case, then who the hell was I? It didn't take me long to make the leap from Jesus to Judas. Obviously, I was bound to meet this person in order to realize that I was, in fact, the reincarnation of Judas Iscariot, the betrayer of Jesus, who—with a kiss on his cheek—turned the Son of God over to the Romans to be crucified. How would you like to live with that guilt? It didn't take me long to realize that I couldn't.

• • •

If I couldn't liberate humanity by reincarnating as Jesus, then the only other option was to *liberate all of humanity* by taking my own life as the reincarnated Judas. After all, Judas had interrupted the mission of the Savior. Now, I had to bow out, eliminate myself from the equation so Jesus, reincarnated as the black soldier, could carry on his mission.

My mind was a Ping-Pong ball of energy, battered back and forth by opposing forces. One second a saint, the next moment a sinner, a reprehensible savage miscreant like Judas, who had turned his back on the world's only true Savior.

The swift transition from Jesus to Judas devastated me. Circuits fried, voltage overloaded, I was paranoia personified. Everyone was obviously *out to get me* because I was the one who had *gotten Jesus*.

There was only one course of action left to redeem everyone on the planet. They were all waiting for me to "do the deed." I could read it in their eyes, in their faces. That demented line of reasoning led me to a disastrous decision a few days later in the dead of night with no one else around.

In the next few days, my paranoia veered off scale. I began to interpret the world, and its inhabitants, in a fatalistic way. Everyone, it was *obvious* to me, was waiting, and had been waiting for eons, for me to realize that I had been Judas. And since I had been the one to betray Christ, the Savior, everyone *but me* had by now been saved. All were saved but the *betrayer*. If they were saved, then why in heaven's name were they still on earth?

The answer became chillingly clear: the only act remaining was for the betrayer to betray himself! Only by my betrayal would the karmic debt I owed Jesus be paid. I, as Judas, was holding everyone hostage here on earth! If only I were to *end my own life*, then all others could instantly and rapturously ascend to heaven!

With my pending self-destruction, it was now clear: the world would disappear as all of us ascended to Heaven. I, too, would be cleansed, purified via self-sacrifice, and sanctified at last.

A succession of thoughts devolved like a wild horse galloping off a cliff. My irrational tangent escalated into a simple, horrifying resolve: **suicide** was the only freedom; self-destruction was the only *constructive* liberation, not only for me, but for all of my fellow souls who had so patiently waited for me to come to this fateful conclusion. After all, they had already earned liberation—maybe years or lifetimes earlier—and had to remain on earth in carnal, flesh bodies for me to awaken to my destiny.

Curiously, I observed all of my mental reasoning with cool reserve, with an aloof, detached objectivity. Previously, I had never entertained the slightest thought of suicide until this apparently fatal sequence of events. Maybe it was the overwhelming guilt about renouncing my religion. Probably it was the drug-induced paranoia or possibly the insanity of war—of watching soldiers blown to pieces before my eyes. Certainly, it was the *Pandora's Box* of past-life fascination, which mesmerized me into hypnotic trance, catapulting my consciousness beyond the borders of sanity.

Whatever the recipe, I was now fully prepared to end my life. At last, I could achieve atonement. It was obvious and inevitable. Preconceived and predetermined. I could clearly read it in the faces of everyone I encountered on the base compound. They were *impatient*. They had waited too long for me to come to the realization that would release them from the tethers of the mundane world.

I saw my future everywhere. Numbers were fatal equations. There were omens, signs in every cloud formation, meal, conversation, phone call, reprimand and interaction. It was the grand, incontrovertible solution: I simply had to kill myself. For everyone else on the planet to be liberated, to reach heaven instantly, I had to make the supreme sacrifice of eliminating myself. It was the only way.

• • •

I entered my telecom hut, a small space three feet by six feet. It had just room enough for the telecom equipment, a swivel chair and waist-high filing cabinets. I set my M-14 rifle on the cabinet, took out a full metal jacket and slapped the ammo into place.

Now that I had made the decision, I was somehow distanced and aloof—separated from the horror of the act—by the clear certainty of my task.

I curiously checked the clock whose hands were at 90 degrees forming 3 A.M.—just the hour Jesus chose to depart the Garden of Gethsemane on his way to being betrayed by Judas.

I picked up the weapon, my sanity slipping over the edge of a cliff, free falling with cool detachment into a macabre nightmare of despair. Lost in a void of illusion, my thoughts fluttered like ribbons blowing in a witch's wind, a madcap cackle of lunacy. My world had shrunk to this small cubicle I would never walk out of alive again.

I turned the rifle around and placed the cold steel barrel, about the circumference of a dime, against the bridge of my nose, right between my eyes. Only seconds away now, I was going to do it . . . alone in the dead of night. The mid-shift meal had been over an hour ago with everyone now back at their posts. I could almost feel the bullet slamming into my frontal lobe, lobotomizing me, mystically exploding my brains into a billion bits of infinity.

I looked around calmly, keenly observing, feeling my blood pulse for the last time.

Closing my eyes . . . my finger resting on the trigger . . . ready now. '*The hour is at hand. You are mine sayeth the Lord. Yea, though I walk through the valley of the shadow of death. I will fear no evil.*' Gently putting the slightest pressure on the trigger, flesh on steel . . . a few ounces more pressure and there would be a pop and a jerk and I would be gone. They would all be liberated. In this way, *I was now the Savior*. My finger on the trigger . . .

. . .

"BANG, BANG, BANG" came a loud knock on my hutch window. I put the rifle down on the filing cabinet. Peaking in, Alberto Gomez opened the door and stepped in, laughing. Having seen me with the gun to my head, he asked, "What're ya trying to do, Baker, kill yourself?"

Checking the chamber, he choked on his gasp, exhaling the words, "Jesus Christ!" He lurched, stumbling out of the room with my rifle in hand, to go find our squad leader, Sergeant Kline. Within minutes, Kline hurried in with another member of our crew, relieving me of duty. Handcuffed, they took me to the Military Police barracks where I sat for the rest of the night wondering what would happen. Wherever I went the next morning and afternoon, an armed MP escorted me.

After 36 hours under line-of-sight guard, the MPs informed me that I was on my way home to the USA! They would put me on a plane within hours.

A brief flight took me to Vung Tau Airbase, where they ushered me into a medical facility. Two men in white coats and pleasant smiles inquired as to why I was there. I replied, "For no reason at all. I'm fine. This is obviously a place for crazy people!"

"Then why don't you go home?" one of them asked, innocently.

"I thought I was—*and I think I will*," I confirmed, standing to shake their hands profusely. I walked out, heading toward the airstrip at the end of the compound.

"That was easy," I thought to myself. I exhaled a sigh of relief—then four men accosted me from behind, two MPs and the two men I had just bade farewell. Quickly subduing me, they led me back to a small cell where I spent the night. The straitjacket was removed about an hour later when they brought in food.

During the meal, two doctors convinced me I would be staying with them a few days for observation and just to treat the whole experience as some "R & R" (army jargon for "rest and recuperation"). Their calm, reassuring words, and the hot meal, helped me gain perspective on my situation.

Gradually, I realized this was some type of recovery unit for military personnel who had either been wounded in combat, or had encountered mental difficulties in coping with the trauma of war.

After being assigned my bunk and hospital attire, I quickly acclimated to the daily routine. There were regular meals—the usual bland military food—exercise time, the recreation room for Ping-Pong, pool or TV . . . and the dreaded *therapy*.

Every afternoon, our group of twelve men would congregate in a conference room for group therapy. No one had to talk, but each of us was encouraged to share why we were here, what our circumstances were and, most importantly, what we thought we might have to do in order to leave.

Before I share some embarrassing situations, which occurred both at therapy and in our hospital unit, let me just say that *it wasn't normal here.* Events transpiring around me were *otherworldly.* For example, returning from breakfast one morning, I spotted a plane, probably just a thousand feet up. My jaw dropped as I observed the speed of the large aircraft, a C-137 troop carrier. Or should I say *lack of speed.* The plane was flying in slow motion! It wasn't just slow . . . it was *barely moving*—defying the laws of gravity! I felt as if I were either in a dream or a science fiction movie.

Later that night, as I was taking a shower, I washed my genital area. There was no feeling or sensation between my legs. Thankfully, I have always had an active libido. No problems, hesitations, or lack of response. On this occasion, oddly, I felt like I was washing my earlobe or my kneecap—no sensitivity *at all!* It was as if I was in some stranger's body—one that didn't work!

I hadn't paid too much attention to the other patients at this facility, but on the way back to my bunk, I happened to notice one. He was resting in his bed, with railing up on the sides, gawking at me with a big smile on his face. I nodded politely, observing the rest of him on my way past. He looked like an extra-terrestrial! His limbs were inhumanly thin, far too elongated, and in no way could support the frame of more than a stickman. Resembling pictures of the inmates at a Nazi concentration camp, this man either had only moments to live . . . or I was in *some other dimension*!

Hiding my feelings, I walked on, blood draining from my face, and occasionally glanced at the other bunks in the dorm. Aside from the others, who were in various stages of their evening, some in clothes and some already in pajamas, there were quite a few who just looked *weird* to me. Some had heads too large, or had animal or bird-shaped heads. On some of these strange bodies, the limbs were contorted into geometrically odd shapes, more like pretzels than people. Suddenly paranoid, I felt eyes watching my back and quickly moved to my bunk, which was in an open dorm setting.

Believing this to be some astral realm or limbo for lost souls, seeing these unworldly beings, and the earlier events of the day, I didn't bother to shield myself from the nearby nurses as I dropped the towel and slowly put on my nightshirt. The closest nurse gave me a big smile, watching what she thought was a show. I knew better. Or so I thought.

The next day at group therapy, our psychiatrist, Dr. Fidelio, made the usual rounds of asking members to share feelings. Instantly, I flashed on his name: *Fidelio*. I knew from my Latin studies in high school that *fidelio* was the root word for our English word *fidelity*, meaning truth or trust.

To me it was an epiphany—I *could now* resolve the situation, the reason for my being here, with a simple act of trust. Judas betrayed Jesus with a kiss on the cheek. If I truly had been the despised Judas, perhaps I could redeem myself with a similar kiss. On impulse, I rose from my seat, walked over to Dr. Fidelio, leaned in and kissed his cheek. No words were spoken, and I returned to my seat, relieved. I was righting a wrong of 2,000 years!

No one said anything. The others ignored my act and so did the doctor. What was I to do? Was it a dream . . . had I not just admitted my guilt of my former self and bestowed this historical kiss, again, in front of witnesses? Love me or hate me, but *don't ignore me*!

I waited a few minutes for a reaction. Finally, after more anxious moments, I realized the only sane thing to do was to *do it again*. Dr. Fidelio was conversing with someone when I again approached him. As I leaned down to plant another kiss on his cheek, he raised his hand in protest.

"You don't need to do that anymore," he said gently. "Why don't you just go back to your seat?"

A flood of emotion filled me as I sat down, relieved at finally having had some acknowledgment.

• • •

The rest of the week went smoothly. By the third day of therapy, I made a few acquaintances, realizing some of these men were in desperate need of help. I, of course, was here *by mistake*—so I played the game of parroting back the answers I knew they wanted to hear. Soon, they were quite pleased with my apparent *improvement* and scheduled my return to my unit in Soc Trang.

First, I stopped talking the gibberish they didn't want to hear—about karma, reincarnation, Jesus, Judas, and the end of the world. I shared about my family, how I missed them, the stress I had been under, what I wanted to do when I got out of the Army, how I desired to resume my schooling. They were overjoyed with *their* success with my therapeutic process.

Then more bewilderment: The night prior to my deployment back to my unit, I was reassigned to a barracks closer to the airfield. I had a good sleep, woke up, had breakfast, packed my duffel bag and headed to the airfield. When I checked in, they said the wait would be about an hour. I asked if they had anything to read. The lady at the desk pointed to a bookshelf filled with magazines and a few books. I smiled a thank you and sat down.

I picked up a book and opened it. My eyes widened as I looked closely. The words were in English, but the text and punctuation were wrong. Sentences were ending halfway through, with periods and commas placed inappropriately. One couldn't follow the writer's thoughts with this kind of editing. I flipped through a few more pages—all the same. Was it a joke? I laughed and replaced the book in the shelf, taking out another. Opening it at random, I was stunned to see the same type of errors, omissions and dereliction of grammatical duty. How could anyone be expected to read, enjoy or comprehend under these circumstances? I looked at a few more books, refusing to believe they could all be as cockeyed, discordant and incorrect as the first two.

Shaking my head, I saw they were all similarly distorted. The words didn't even follow in logical sequence. I picked up a *Reader's Digest*. Everyone knows *Reader's Digest!* That had to be

OK. Same insanity—oh, sure, the articles each had titles and subtitles, but when I started reading a story, it was all gibberish again. Nonsensical absurdity! I tossed it aside, storming over to the lady who checked me in for my flight.

"Ma'am, excuse me, but none of the books over there make any sense!" I blurted out, not knowing how else to say it. "All the punctuation's wrong—it's all gobbledygook!"

She looked at me with kind eyes and a weak smile.

"I'm sorry, but that's all we have to read," she said.

Getting nowhere, I inquired about my flight.

"It should be here any time now," she said, glad to change the subject.

I thanked her, went back to sit by the bookshelf, looked through a few more of the puzzling magazines and books—just to make sure I hadn't been hallucinating—and threw each one down in disgust. Instead of plain English, they appeared to be configured in some secret code, and I didn't have a clue!

Another half hour, then another hour went by without any news of my flight. Each time I asked about it, she politely gave me the same answer.

"It should be arriving any time now." Finally, at 4pm, I got angry.

"But Ma'am, you've been telling me that *all day—where the hell is it?*"

She asked me to wait a moment, went over to check with a supervisor, and promptly returned.

"I am very sorry, but that flight had mechanical trouble. We just found out about it, so they will have to send another one tomorrow. There are no more flights out today," she said, with eyes that hoped I wouldn't explode.

I dropped my shoulders, took a deep breath, thanked her in a barely audible tone, and walked over to grab my gear and head for the barracks. When I got there, more bad news. They informed me my place had been filled with a new arrival. I would have to seek quarters elsewhere.

"Damn!" I whispered under my breath, striding away. Outside, I lit a Kool and gazed around. Feeling alienated and abandoned, I watched dusk darken over this day from hell.

. . .

After wandering around several other barracks and being told they, too, were full, I finally gave up and went to the mess tent for dinner. Midway through the meal, another soldier sat down next to me. After explaining my predicament, he told me his friend just checked out that afternoon and he was sure there was a place for me. He was correct. For once, I had been in the right place at the right time.

Returning from breakfast between two barracks the next morning, a man approached me saying, "You want to get a flight out of here, right?"

Bewildered at how this stranger would know my status, when he hadn't even asked my name, I hesitated for a moment and then said, "Well, yeah."

"Okay," he quickly informed, "the airfield you want to fly out of is on the other side of the tower, not the one you were at yesterday. It's the North Field, and there's a flight leaving in fifteen minutes. Can you hustle over there right away?" he asked, more like a command.

"Yes, Sir!" I barked. Thanking him profusely, I ran to the barracks, shouldered my duffel bag and jogged to the airfield he indicated.

As he promised, it went smoothly. I checked in and was informed there would be only a few minutes wait. I took one step toward the waiting area and turned back.

"Ma'am," I asked, "do you by any chance have *something to read*?"

She twisted her mouth to one side, wrinkling her lips in thought.

"I am very sorry," she apologized, "about the only thing we have around here is a dictionary."

That might be all I would need.

"That's fine," I said. "Mind if I take a look?"

She smiled, lugging the large, oversized volume in both hands.

I eagerly carried it to a nearby seat, opened it somewhere toward the middle, and scanned a few words. I was pleased to see that the definitions were accurate, the punctuation correct—that *logic* was back in my world!

Opening the dictionary to another section, my eyes landed on a word that seemed to jump off the page. It was **solipsism**, a psychological term meaning: "someone who believes that he is the *only person in the world*." It was the epitome of how I had been feeling!

A moment later, the lady at the desk interrupted my reverie: "Private Baker, your flight is ready. You may board."

A few weeks after redeployment to my unit, my year in Viet Nam was up. I returned to the USA, served my last six months of active duty in Florida without incident and mustered out of the Army. Ironically, I was released on the 4th of July—independence! Free at last!

CHAPTER 2

Rooms in the Mansion

I like this biblical quote attributed to Jesus, which expresses a key principle. In John 14:2, Jesus says, "In my Father's House are many mansions." To carry this analogy further, we could add, "and in those mansions are many rooms." Each room in our mind is a state of consciousness. The point I'm making here is that suicide is just a room in the mansion—and you or someone you love may be in that room right now. The freedom we have as human beings is to either stay in a room, or leave and enter another room. That "other" room may be to finish the rest of your life and see what happens. At any time, at any moment in your life, you can choose to go in or out of any room in the mansion of your mind.

That's the freedom and the power you have. No one can take it away from you.

The rest of my life, after I was saved from suicide, included many new *rooms*. After I finished my two years with the U.S. Army, I went into the room of being a college student again. My failures at the university level meant I had to return to community college and improve my grades. The next room was returning to a four-year university and completing all courses to earn my degree. To accomplish this I had to go into the room of being a dedicated student, doing homework, attending classes and participating so I could earn enough credits to graduate. I did. And it made me feel good about myself. True, I had failed in the past, due to drugs, alcohol and being irresponsible, but now I was succeeding. This was all new for me because I wasn't used to success.

I earned a Bachelor of Arts degree in English Literature, followed by a teaching credential, which took another year, and eventually earned a Master's Degree in English & American Literature. During this period, I married my college sweetheart and eventually we had two wonderful daughters, who are now 51 and 47 and have children of their own—my grandchildren! I never would have had all this if I had committed suicide back in 1967.

Since I didn't have a lot or money after my stint in the Army, I had to go into the room of earning income so I could pay for my college education. The many jobs I took were varied and interesting. I was a switchman for the railroad, a night watchman for a mortuary, an assistant in the Hematology (blood) Lab at a hospital for those with intellectual disabilities, a group supervisor on the night shift at Central Juvenile Hall in Los Angeles, sorting mail at the main post office downtown L.A., and many other jobs. I even mopped classroom floors at night for a school district. Later, after I earned my teaching credential, I was able to have a seven-year career as a high school English and Art teacher. Following this was a successful fifteen-year career in real estate. Other careers followed in sales & marketing while I pursued writing and art.

Like many people, I went through the room of divorce after a dozen years of marriage with my first wife. Eventually, after a few years of being single, I magically found another wonderful woman—wife, lover, best friend and partner—to share my life. We have been together for over thirty-five years.

CHAPTER 3

Near Death Experiences

As I mentioned above, once my near death experience with suicide was aborted by what I call *Divine Intervention,* I let go of the idea of taking my own life. It was far too miraculous and jolted me out of the journey which had led me to thoughts of suicide. In writing this book, I began to reflect on many other close calls I had with other NDEs—Near Death Experiences.

The first one I recall was when I had a paper route as a teenager. I was fourteen and had an afternoon route near the USC campus in Los Angeles. I had to cross a major boulevard, Hoover Street, to get to and from the neighborhoods where I delivered newspapers. One afternoon, after throwing my papers, I was riding back along Hoover. I saw there was no oncoming traffic—and didn't hear any behind me—so I rode across the intersection. Suddenly, I heard the squeal of brakes and a blaring horn. I made it across safely, but the honking car, a four-door sedan, ended up screeching to a halt in the lanes of oncoming traffic, which, fortunately, there was none. No one was injured. The couple in the car told me to wait while they parked. They demanded my address, which was a few blocks away. Minutes later, I walked in our front door; the couple was sitting in our living room, speaking with my parents. Yes, I got a good lecture after the couple left, but not the spanking I expected. My parents were too happy to know I was alive and uninjured. Once again, I had been saved. Was it divine intervention—somebody "upstairs" watching out for me? Who knows? Maybe this timely book is the way someone is watching out for you.

• • •

My next NDE took place during my college years. I was in a fraternity and we drank hard and often. Although never diagnosed or officially labeled, I was certainly an alcoholic. One night, right before I was turning in for the night, my roommate and fraternity brother, Tom, suddenly arrived from Santa Barbara where he had just broken up with his girlfriend. We started drinking from a huge bottle of cheap wine, and soon were on our way in my old VW bug to a sorority party in a nearby city. As we were speeding through a residential part of Alhambra, he suddenly yelled, "I think it's that way. TURN LEFT!"

I yanked the steering wheel to the left, sending my car onto its wheels on the right side. It continued on over, rolling onto a perfect parking space a few inches from the curb. Tom thought I was dead, as I had passed out, but I awoke a few seconds later. I can still see the sparks flying off the ground as the top of my car rolled end over end. It was a close call, reckless and irresponsible. Definitely flirting with death once again.

Another NDE took place on an airplane runway during my year in Vietnam. A buddy and I were out on the tarmac smoking a joint. We were far away from any aircraft and at a vantage point where we could see anyone who might be approaching. About as safe as one could be, right? No! Within minutes, I heard a "KA-CHING" rocketing past my right ear. Sure enough, an enemy sniper, hiding out in the rice paddies a few hundred feet away on this bright sunny afternoon, had tried to take me out. I shared the news with by friend, not sure if he had heard the sound. We both started jogging, and then running at full speed back toward the relative safety of our barracks. In this case, I had come a few inches from being a military casualty of war.

As in the first instance with rolling my VW, there were too many more NDEs where alcohol played a role. On a number of occasions, primarily in my college years, I was a drunk driver. Like many of those under the influence, I foolishly felt sober enough to drive home. On one occasion, I was pulled over by the police and booked overnight for swerving back and forth through the streets of Alhambra. That resulted in a night in jail. My father had to drive from Torrance the next morning to bail me out. He completely understood because he, too, had been an alcoholic but was able to break his addiction by attending Alcoholics Anonymous (AA) meetings a few times when he was in his 40s. He maintained his sobriety until he died at 89. He was a true role model for me in letting go of my addiction to alcohol.

The next NDE due to a drunk driving episode involved meeting up with buddies from college. We visited a few bars. By the time I got on the freeway to head home, it was after midnight. I was seeing three white lines where there was just one, but I miraculously made it back to my uncle's home in Downey, where I was staying at the time to attend a nearby college.

As frightening and dangerous as my NDEs were, the most terrifying event with my car had nothing to do with alcohol. My father worked for years selling advertising for a newspaper in Culver City, a suburb of Los Angeles. The company eventually built a new facility in nearby Torrance, changing the paper's name to the South Bay Daily Breeze. My overnight job, arranged by my father, was to stand guard at the old newspaper offices while the trucks took everything to the new facility. I was a night watchman, paid to stay awake and alert until morning while everything was transferred to the new offices.

I took the job because the pay was excellent. The problem for me was that I had never stayed up all night in my life. Thus, on the morning drive home, about forty-five minutes mostly on the freeway, I began to fall asleep. I splashed water on my face, slapped my face and sang songs, sometimes shouting them, just to keep awake. I was terrified and several times actually went to sleep while driving, only to pop awake moments later, amazed that I hadn't run the car off the road. I always seemed to miraculously awaken at just the right time to avoid disaster. This panic went on for a good half hour as I fought sleep to save my life.

Here, again, was divine intervention. The Powers That Be, God, Guardian Angels, Spirit Guides or whatever you want to call them saved my life. Why? It's a great question. Why are some saved and others not? Maybe I had some mission or special task that I was to fulfill. Who knows? Maybe that mission was to write this book so you don't have to commit suicide. I hope so. After all, how did you happen to get your hands on *Suicide Survivor* in the first place? As unexpected or strange as it may have occurred, I'm betting it wasn't an accident. It's worth considering that it might just be your second chance at life—to avoid self-sabotage and take a look at what the rest of your life might become. And keep this in mind: with the right training, there is virtually no end to the possibilities that life may have in store for you. Your future is unlimited!

PART II

How to Survive Suicide

CHAPTER 4

Suicide Survivor

Fortunately, I survived suicide. In a miraculous twist of fate, someone stepped in with only seconds to spare to save my life. Whether I wanted to or not, I became a *Suicide Survivor*. You, too, can survive suicide. What I'm hoping is that this book and my story are the catalyst, the impetus or reason that helps you decide to continue living your precious life.

As I said at the start, "there's a lot you don't know about the rest of your life." What I didn't know about the rest of my life was that I would go on to live a long, productive and enjoyable life (I am 80 as of this writing).

Okay, but let's assume that this book *isn't* the final event that changes your mind. There can be many other events or people—friends, even strangers, counselors, books, movies—or other situations that could allow you or convince you to move away from the feeling that suicide is the only answer. As the main character on the TV series, *Ted Lasso*, says, "Be curious, not judgmental." Be *curious* about what might happen in your future instead of being *judgmental* and sentencing yourself with a life ending decision now.

For me, it was instantaneous. As soon as my attempt was interrupted, I knew suicide was not my answer. The timing was too miraculous, utterly amazing. You, however, since you might not have attempted anything drastic yet, might change your mind after reading some of the stories and suggestions starting on page 91. At least the book might play a part in your decision to turn away from the dangerous thoughts you may have now and continue on with the rest of your life. After all, it just could actually turn out to be a long, happy, productive and enjoyable journey. Why not? Why not you? Why not now? A lot depends on your attitude. You always have the power to change your mind.

Could I predict with certainty or guarantee that I would experience joy, happiness, family, marriage, children, or a successful career? No, surely not, but I at least *had a chance* to develop these qualities. Whereas, if you give up now, and take the final plunge, then you definitely won't experience any of the above blessings, experiences, achievements and pleasures that a long, healthy life can bring.

As the amazing basketball star, Michael Jordan, famously said years ago: "I miss 100% of the shots I don't take!" The message was that if you want to make the basket—succeed in life—you must take a chance, take lots of chances, in order to make lots of baskets! In other words, one cannot have a successful life by interrupting it with suicide. Stop judging yourself. Stick around and see what happens. And be sure to read the section about your miraculous brain and body toward the end of the book!

The other thing to consider is that there is no rush here for you. You do not have to "push the river." No need to decide today whether or not you turn the lights out for the last time. Give life (God?) a chance to deliver more reasons or evidence why you should delay or postpone your pending self-imposed death sentence. After all, you could do it on some other day, month or even another year—or never! A delay gives you a chance to gain more perspective about what you are going through. This could be from friends, family, professional counselors or from something new you read or learn.

CHAPTER 5

Why Good People Commit Suicide

"If life happens to throw you a dagger, you can either catch it by the blade or by the handle."

Norman Vincent Peale

People commit suicide for a wide range of reasons. It depends on what is important to each person and how he or she reacts to loss or change. People get fired, lose their income, crash their cars (like I did several times), flunk out of college (like I did several times), have their hearts broken by lovers or divorced by spouses (like I did several times). Others drink too much (like I did way too often), or have eating disorders or get arrested, even spending time in prison. A delicate issue is a change of sexual orientation. I've recently heard that 60% of the suicides of gay young adults occur in the first six months after they come out.

And depression—a trigger to suicide—arises out of pain. The types of suicide are complex. There is intentional suicide, unintentional or accidental suicide, such as a drug overdose (Michael Jackson, Whitney Houston, Prince), and gradual suicide (drug and alcohol abuse, including smoking). For example, smoking can take many years, but it still kills between 500,000 to a million Americans per year.

Then there's food. Can a donut kill you? Death by chocolate? Although this may sound funny, many people end up at death's door *because of their diet.* If we're living on sugary drinks and fast food, there's a good chance our health is being compromised. This can affect our mood and emotions. A diet heavy in drugs, alcohol and sugar can result in extreme mood swings and depression.

Pain can be physical, emotional, psychological or a combination of all three, but it is so intense that the person in distress eventually, after all other remedies fail, considers suicide.

Any of these situations can overwhelm us. Also, one or more of these things happen to just about everyone at some time during their lives. Someone wisely said, "Don't spend too much time blaming yourself and beating yourself up because the rest of the world will gladly do it for you." What many people come to realize is that it is not so important what happens to you because much of it you can't control. What is far more important is *how you react to it.* If life throws you a dagger, catch it by the handle—not the blade! If you catch it by the handle, then you are in control and can change the outcome. Regardless of what happens to you, use it as a stepping-stone to help you grow.

CHAPTER 6

Divine Intervention

Let's talk about timing. Prior to my experience of being saved from suicide, I would not have believed in the concept of *Divine Intervention.* I figured God has way too much to do running the universe or multiverse, as some scientists are now calling it. But when my life was saved—at the last possible moment as I was about to pull the trigger—I realized much later when I had time to think about it, that something miraculous and profound had occurred. Somehow God, or one of His Angels, got pulled into my crisis. They had to *arrange* certain events and maybe nudge or inspire Alberto Gomez to arrive from wherever he had just been to bang on my door the instant before I pulled the trigger. Divine Intervention. No doubt about it.

• • •

Have you ever considered what impact your suicide would have on your family? They certainly hope you outlive them and continue to have a long, productive and rewarding life. All parents want the best for their children, even though they aren't always capable of letting us know how they feel. I am so grateful that I was saved at the last possible instant from destroying myself because it saved my family from the devastating loss my death would have brought them.

Previously, I had what some call "tunnel vision." All I could see, feel or think about was my impending suicide and how important it was to liberate humanity. It's not that I didn't care about my family. I was simply too overwhelmed and obsessed with my own delusional quest.

Evidently, God didn't want me dead. When I pondered it years later, I realized I had actually tried to kill myself quite a few other times, either consciously or unconsciously—but somebody or something kept stepping in to save me. Why? I'm sure there are many reasons, and I hope one of them was to write this book.

CHAPTER 7

The Tragedy of Early Death

If we follow the pattern of nature, the elders usually die before their children. That's what we all expect, even though it doesn't always happen that way. I have a couple of tragic examples. I grew up the youngest of three brothers. Edwin, or "Buck" as we called him, was the oldest. Then came Bobby, two years later, and I was the youngest, in another two years. We had a nice family. My dad and mom both worked. We weren't rich by any means, but we always had the mortgage paid and food on the table. We took travel vacations in the summer.

Buck was a genius. Literally. With an exceptionally high IQ, he spoke several languages and was granted a full scholarship to Loyola University in Los Angeles. However, it didn't suit him.

He was too interested in his own pursuits to study the college curriculum. He was a voracious reader from an early age. He read everything. One passion was science fiction, and he became president of LASFS, the Los Angeles Science Fiction Society. He was also fluent in Esperanto, an artificially created language that was devised to help unify the world. He had pen pals from many countries with whom he communicated regularly. Unfortunately, he lost his scholarship due to poor grades and had to drop out of college and seek employment.

He got a job with an insurance company and held seminars to explain the company's benefits. One night he gave a presentation in South Central Los Angeles. As he was driving away from the neighborhood after the meeting, a couple stepped close at a stop sign and pulled a gun on him—what we now call a carjacking. Buck tried to speed away but shots were fired. The car crashed nearby and he died at the scene. He was only 29.

We were devastated. As I mentioned, this wasn't the normal order of things. This wasn't the way life was supposed to happen, but as we all learn eventually, you can't argue with fate or death. You just go on doing the best you can. Bobby and I mourned the loss of our brother. As children, Buck and I often fought, but as I got older I learned to appreciate his wonderful qualities. He had a good heart and was very loving to us in his own, unique way. As stunned and numb as I was with his sudden passing, it was comforting for me to have already learned about reincarnation while in Vietnam. Even though these concepts sent me on a possibly fatal line of reasoning whereby I almost killed myself, they later helped me navigate the circumstances surrounding my brother's death.

• • •

The next part of my life that exemplifies the tragedy of early death has to do with my son, Kris Murray. Kris had identity issues from day one—actually from nine months prior to day one. For starters, he wasn't planned.

I had ended my first marriage on November 1 of 1984. On Thanksgiving, a few weeks later, I was invited to a friend's family for the customary dinner. At the event, I met Marina, the niece of the woman my good friend was dating at the time. Marina and I began seeing each other a few weeks later. The first time we got into bed, she said, "Oh . . . I forgot my birth control."

I casually said, "Don't worry about it. If we have a child, we have a child."

As fate would have it, my cavalier attitude backfired. Although our relationship was short-lived and we broke up on Valentine's Day, 1985, just ten weeks later, we soon learned that Marina was pregnant. At the time, I wasn't ready for another child, especially with a woman I had just parted with, so we both agreed she would have an abortion. I asked if she needed financial assistance or to have me with her that day, but she declined, saying she would take care of everything herself. The following day, I called her to see how she was. She affirmed that all had gone well. Soon after,

I moved farther away. Her phone number was disconnected and months went by.

About six months later, I heard she had met someone new and was pregnant again. After that baby was born, her aunt, who was still dating my friend, called and suggested I go see Marina, hinting that there was much Marina hadn't shared with me.

Around that time, I had to travel to San Diego to renew my real estate license, so I made a point of visiting Marina on my return trip. Sure enough, there was Kris, a brand new baby. Point blank, I asked her, "Whose baby is it? Am I the father?"

Her nonchalant reply was evasive. She said it was *her baby* and that she wasn't sure who the father was because while she was dating me, she was dating others as well. She was cold and aloof. We parted without her divulging that the baby *was*, in fact, mine—which she eventually did a year and a half later, apologizing for withholding the truth for so long.

Earlier, I mentioned that Kris' last name was Murray. That surname came from a man Marina met in the months before Kris was born. She believed that she and Mr. Murray were going to be married, but that relationship didn't last. Kris's birth certificate had Murray as his father. I tried for years to have that changed, to no avail. Later, Marina married a man named Benson. For simplicity's sake, my son was known as Kris Benson from then on. So, while I am his biological father, with a last name of Baker, his legal name was always Murray by school administrators, and then

Benson by friends and family. I'm sure a child growing up with this identity confusion has to say, "Who exactly am I?"

Marina developed a drug problem and was eventually incarcerated. Kris and his sister Rachel Benson were placed with Child Protection Services. Later, he came to live with my wife and me. At that stage in his young life, Kris was bitter, rebellious and had become addicted to marijuana. In time, his mother was released and had moved to within ten miles of us. Kris lived with us during the week and spent weekends with his mother and Lane, her boyfriend. In his freshman year of high school, just prior to first period, he was caught carrying a loaded 22-caliber handgun that he had stolen from Lane. The rest of his high school years were spent in and out of rehabilitation programs and juvenile hall. After turning eighteen, he even spent a couple of weeks in adult prison. He had borrowed his mother's leather jacket—not realizing her hunting knife was in a pocket. He was charged with carrying a concealed weapon.

We believe adult prison scared him enough to change his ways. He soon apprenticed with Lane, who owned a thriving business servicing and repairing microscopes in scientific and high-tech offices around the county. Adept at using his hands for detail work, Kris soon became proficient in the business. He began to save his earnings, garnering some much-needed self-esteem along the way. He got a pit-bull and learned guitar online. He later restored a Mazda, taking the entire engine apart and putting it back together. Although he never did graduate from high school, his vocabulary expanded rapidly as he learned the language of automobiles and the scientific terms in the science labs and police offices where he serviced microscopes.

By his early twenties, Kris had saved enough to purchase a motorcycle. He loved his "bike" and took pride in his ability to weave in and out of traffic, cutting back and forth like a daredevil on the freeway with what appeared to be careless abandon. Unfortunately, he also liked to socialize with his widening circle of friends and have a few drinks. In the early hours of November 12, 2011, after a party, Kris and his best friend Keith headed home on their motorcycles, traveling through a residential area of Oceanside, California. At the last possible moment, a van pulled out from a side street, blocking their path. Keith was on the inside and able to swerve around the van. Kris, however, crashed head on into the van and died instantly: Another tragic death of a young man—my son—with his whole life seemingly ahead of him.

I had plans for Kris. He had become an expert mechanic and I loved classic cars. I dreamed of opening a classic car restoration business with Kris as my partner, but it wasn't to be. He had apparently learned everything he needed to learn in this life as Kris Murray Benson Baker. His sudden, unexpected death caught us by surprise. We were stunned, devastated and in shock, of course, but these things happen. You have to move on, treasuring the good times and the special memories. Nonetheless, my understanding of karma and reincarnation helped me again to process Kris' passing, just as it had with my brother's death.

Even though these stories are sad, I hope they inspire you because there is nothing more terrible than a life cut short by a tragic, unexpected death. If by now you, or someone you love, is still living a potentially suicidal life, I hope you or they will reconsider. Whether you know it or not, there are many people rooting for you, hoping you live out all your years to their natural conclusion, which can be decades from now. Remember, *"There's a whole lot you don't know about the rest of your life!"*

What I found, though, was the longer time went on, the more distance I had from that fateful day when I almost committed suicide, the happier I became. Life had opened up for me. I started to read, amazed at how many characters, plots and worlds were out there, waiting to be discovered. I grew to understand myself better by the various viewpoints expressed in fiction. I found that many of the situations they faced were similar to mine. I wasn't the "lone ranger," stuck in some terrible dilemma with no way out. I learned that I had options, choices, and a certain degree of freedom that was liberating and enjoyable. Life became a quest, an adventure, a journey, a daily opportunity to discover more about this life I was living. I became hungry for more knowledge instead of constantly judging myself. I let go of those self-destructive thoughts and began to see life more as a series of opportunities to be taken advantage of. I gradually learned from leaders in the human potential movement that the greatest thing I had, which could impact my future, was my attitude.

• • •

Earlier, I touched on the idea of *states of consciousness*. It's similar to the "room" idea. Our consciousness is made up of all that we have ever experienced, all that we know or believe or have been taught. A state of consciousness is similar to a state in our United States. Here's an example: A person from California will have a California consciousness and a person from Texas will have a Texas consciousness. Years ago, the famous rocker Billy Joel wrote and performed a song entitled, "New York State of Mind." He understood this principle.

What I'm getting at here is that suicide is a state—a state of consciousness—that you can leave. Just as you can be in California one day and in Texas the next, you can also leave the state of suicide behind, shifting into any other state of mind you choose. The one freedom we will always have is the power to change our mind, which is to change our state of consciousness.

CHAPTER 8

How to Avoid Suicide

Sometimes a change of scenery can change your life. When I got out of the army, I left all that turmoil in Vietnam. I reconnected with my family in Los Angeles, which brought a sense of stability to my life. I went back to school and got a job. Everything was brand new. I had a fresh start. Lots of new rooms were opening up. There was so much to live for now than to think about dying.

The way to avoid suicide—if you really are looking for a way out—is to "go into another room." It could mean going into the room of having a more positive attitude. It could be the room of deciding to learn guitar or some other musical instrument. It could be the room of education—going back to school, going into rehab, or just reading a novel or a self-help book. It could also mean getting some help with a physical or psychological problem. There are plenty of rooms in the mansion of your mind that can take you out of the suicide room. You can open any and all of the rooms you wish to visit. Another way to look at this room analogy is to see that you also have the power to lock yourself out of the suicide room. You alone hold the key! Be sure to review the resources listed and explained below in the Appendix to determine which action steps you can take now.

In the film, *Matrix Resurrection,* Neal Patrick Harris, the character of The Analyst tells Neo, played by Keanu Reeves, "You are a *Suicide Survivor* . . ." This sentence is an example of serendipity. Some call it a divine message in that it had no relation to me in the movie but had profound importance to me personally. Why? Because I had been pondering the idea of writing a book about my year in Vietnam.

Specifically, I would recount my near-death experience with suicide. I had envisioned the book's title as *Suicide Survivor.* So, when Neal Patrick Harris uttered the very same words in the film, it was a wake-up call for me—a call to action: Write a book about my story and share it with others. I have a simple goal. If my book can save one person from committing suicide, it will be well worth it. I sincerely hope that person is you or someone you love.

The rest of *your* life, presupposing you take a step back from that ledge or put down the gun, will have a lot of common denominators with the rest of humanity. If we look at statistics, most people have a series of jobs or careers throughout their lives, and many different types of families with a wide variety of family dynamics. Also, you will most likely engage in several romantic relationships, maybe a marriage or two. You might have a pet of some kind and enjoy travel around the USA or to other countries. A number of you will own your own home, most of you will own a car, and you will experience a number of healthy and unhealthy lifestyles. To get there you will have to overcome your current challenge—but you are not alone. Many people of all ages have gone through a similar crisis to the one you are experiencing.

PART III

Your Spiritual Life

CHAPTER 9

The Role of Karma and Reincarnation

Why Do Bad Things Happen to Good People? According to karma, known as the Spiritual Law of Cause & Effect, whatever energy you send out into the world will, at some time in the future, come back to you like a boomerang. It is also a Newtonian scientific theory: For every action there is an equal and opposite reaction. Jesus is said to have stated it more simply as recorded in the Bible: "As ye sow, so shall ye reap," a simple reference to farming: If you plant corn, you will grow corn. In real life, if you plant seeds of anger, hatred or revenge, those are the types of situations that will show up in your life. Conversely, if you are putting peace, love, joy and gratitude into your world, then that is exactly what will usually return to you, either now or in the future.

Many of the events that happen in your present life—both positive and negative—may be the result of something you did in a previous life. My brother Buck might have shot or killed someone in another lifetime, and his similar death in this life might have been the boomerang effect, an example of the spiritual law of cause and effect, or karma. It provides a rationale for why bad things happen to good people.

Karma implies reincarnation, and these concepts—you might call them formulas for divine justice—made a lot of sense to me. When I later began to study world religions, I found that 75% of people around the globe believe in the theories of reincarnation with karma.

It's comforting to know that if we make a train wreck of this current life, with suicide for example, it won't be the end of us. The spiritual part of each of us is Soul. And Soul goes on from one lifetime to another, gaining more experience and learning from our mistakes. We might live hundreds or even thousands of lives. Just as we graduate from first grade through eighth grade in school, then are promoted to high school and maybe on to college, I believe we also graduate from Planet Earth and are promoted when we have learned everything we can from our current life on earth. After all, there is a vast universe out there with billions of other planets, which scientists continue to explore.

While the idea of karma and reincarnation did play a role in my suicide attempt, I came to realize why this doctrine is so important. An understanding of these beliefs allows you to come into an acceptance of who you really are, where you have been and where you are going. If you do commit suicide, the law of karma states that you will have to return to earth and go through it all over again under similar circumstances. And it doesn't matter who you *might have been* in a past life. If we do live hundreds or even thousands of lives, then we have lived every type of life one can imagine. The famous singer Frank Sinatra touched on this idea in his hit song, *That's Life*: "I've been a puppet, a pauper, a poet, a pirate . . . a pawn and a king." What is vastly more important is what you have learned from all these lives—and what you can still learn from your life now.

The key point to consider about reincarnation is the idea that each of us has a Soul—or is a Soul. Just as a body wears clothes, but is not the clothing, Soul resides in a body but is not that body. Soul is the true, eternal, indestructible, spiritual part of each of us, which continues on, life after life. It is the everlasting part of us—not the mind, not the emotions, nor the physical body. All of those are important but impermanent. They only last as long as we live in *this* body. Once we die, those bodies are finished. Each person's Soul, however, lives on with stored memories of all past lives, and eventually is given a new life on earth. It returns as a newborn, sometimes as a male, and other times as a female, but with little memory of any prior lives. The slate is clean and we start anew, usually with new lessons to learn.

Some people do have past life memories, but most do not. I have one friend who is Puerto Rican. He is traditional in every other way, except for food. Every week, he must eat some sushi or other Japanese food. In fact, he loves everything Japanese. That is how one might see a past life in Japan manifested in someone's current life.

Writing and art are two important parts of my life, and very probably were activities carried over from some of my past lives. For some, it might be gardening, cooking or dance. For others, it could be the sciences, archeology or climate change. Are you drawn to learning a specific language or traveling to a certain country? If it's Italian, there's a good chance you had a past life in Italy.

Reincarnation means we don't have to learn everything in one lifetime. We have endless opportunities to expand, mature, and evolve on planet earth—and possibly on other planets as well.

With this framework of beliefs, I could grieve and then let my brother go. Sure, he died a tragic death as Edwin "Buck" Baker, but as Soul, indestructible and eternal, he was given a promotion. He graduated. He completed his assignment. There wasn't anything else he had to learn in the life we lived as brothers. And the same goes for my son, Kris. He will reincarnate in due time—or has already—when new conditions are ideal for him/her to enter a family which can provide exactly the life lessons he needs for his ongoing journey throughout eternity, life after life.

It was tragic for our family and always would be, and that's what is overwhelming about early death, such as suicide or fatal accidents. When I was in crisis, I never thought about my family and how terrible my death at only 21 might have been for them. I was so wrapped up in my own bundle of delusions that I didn't consider how emotionally crushed and blindsided they would be. I am so grateful for the time I have spent with my family and for the life I have been able to live all these years—and hopefully many more.

In retrospect, what had thrown me off track from the normal pattern of life was a series of what I term "thought forms," leading me on a tangent away from the reality of my normal, sane, logical, daily routine. Psychologists might term this condition as illusion or delusion. Mystics call it *The Dark Night of the Soul.*

CHAPTER 10

Dark Night of the Soul

The Dark Night of the Soul happens when everything seems to go wrong at the same time: physical, emotional, and psychological problems pile up, which may include finances, career or relationships. It can be so bad it seems like there is no way out. Would it surprise you to know that some of this happens to everyone from time to time? When it hits you all at once, though, it can be too much to bear. You feel like this avalanche of problems is going to bury you. That's when thoughts of suicide crop up. "I can't take it anymore." "There's no way out." "Put me out of my misery!" "I give up!" "I quit!" You long for that comforting relief of drugs and/or alcohol. And just like that, you're veering off course. Thoughts of ending it all seep into your brain like weeds in the cracks of a sidewalk.

But do we really want to die—or just escape the torture life has become? It's an important question to answer—*which may just save your life.*

Have you ever felt this way, that too many bad things are stacked up against you and you just can't go on living? The classic examples are found in the lyrics of Country & Western songs. The cowboy comes home from his job on the ranch to find his wife has run off with his best friend. Not only that but she stole his truck and took their dog. The next day he loses his job and someone steals his horse. A few days later his house burns down. It goes on and on. Finally, on a gloomy day, he looks up into the sky with tears in his eyes and begs, "God, *please* tell me why all these terrible things keep happening to me?"

Instantly, the clouds part and God's thundering voice booms, "I don't know . . . there's just something about you that pisses me off!" While it is an amusing story because God would never behave that way—at least I don't think so—sometimes it feels like we are getting all the bad luck piled on so high it crushes us.

The truth of this matter is that as good or bad as life gets, there are always people who have it better or worse. Millions of people around this world are homeless and hungry. A good way to deal with your problems is to focus on something or someone else. Take the attention off of yourself. I heard a member of the clergy recently say: "Stop telling God how big your problems are and start telling your problems how big your God is!"

When everything begins to snowball into an avalanche, that's when it's time to step back, reassess and put things into perspective. Do some journaling, meet a friend for coffee, take the day off, and maybe explore a nearby city. If you pray, contemplate or meditate, now's the time to do it. Once you feel better, here are some ways to shift the attention away from yourself and away from your problems: Do volunteer work. Go to a local church or community center. Offer to spend a few hours every week at a local food pantry. Work at an animal shelter. Find ways to be of service, making life easier for someone else, even if it is just a smile, holding the door for an elderly person, or sharing food with the homeless. Any of these activities shift your attention off of yourself. Recall the theory of karma. When you are being of service to others, you are setting the stage for others to be of service to you. There is no greater feeling in the world than to help others in need. When you do that, you are helping yourself as well.

CHAPTER 11

You Are Unique

If someone were to ask me what spiritual gold I have discovered this lifetime, I would have to say it is reading. Yes, those first ten books on Tibetan Buddhism set the stage for my spiral downward, but reading also brought me back up. It provided many new and exciting stories, which helped me grow and expand in consciousness. *Learning* itself became a spiritual experience to which there was no end in sight. It allowed me to find and explore many new religions and spiritual paths until I found the one that was right for me—one that included *everyone*. I came to realize that God was incomplete without me—and everyone else! No one was left behind without another chance to graduate from planet Earth.

I was surprised to learn that on a genetic level, all human beings are more than 99% identical. However, what is unique about each of us is that no one else in the history of the world will have had the same unique pattern of lifetimes, circumstances and experiences as you. No one will have the same exact combination of viewpoints, attitudes or beliefs as you. Not even identical twins! Many may have similar experiences, but none in the same exact order. That makes each of us unique in all the history of the world. Because of that, no one can really judge you or your behavior since you are the only one living your life in your own unique way. Sure, they can *attempt* to judge you, but you are the only one who knows exactly what it feels like to be you.

Accordingly, that means you aren't in a position to judge anyone else either. I believe we're all doing the best we can, each moment of every day. We might do better next time, but for this moment, we couldn't really have done anything other than what we did, based on everything we knew and felt and believed at that moment. We will most likely improve next time because we will have more experience. When I realized the truth of these thoughts, I felt liberated. I was no longer chased around by a belief that I wasn't worthy. I began to *value* myself. And it's not vanity or ego. It's a recognition of who I really am—a divine Soul, just like each and everyone else!

If we are truly unique—and I believe each and every one of us is—then we will have certain goals and dreams that only we can achieve. If you want to pursue your goals, cutting your life short is not an option. And you're not alone. Like you, and thousands of others around the world, I faced overwhelming forces pointing me toward self-destruction. Fortunately, my Guardian Angel was working overtime!

CHAPTER 12

The Miracle of the Human Body

Juggling thoughts of suicide is gambling with your life. Are you willing to take that risk? Let's take a survey of what's at stake. What exactly is involved with this human body—namely *your* human body—that is in jeopardy?

Let's explore this awe-inspiring creation that is a human being. Nothing else in the universe is quite like it! Our body is delicate yet powerful, incredibly complex but at times amazingly simple. It is a masterpiece of nature's engineering, a symphony of complexity and resilience. Its thirty-seven trillion cells work tirelessly, constantly renewing and adapting.

Our body is a wonderland: A unique, miraculous operating system. Yes, it's disgusting at times, but that is the way our bodies keep us in balance and healthy.

The heart, a tireless warrior, beats over three billion times during an average human lifespan. It pumps 2,000 gallons of blood daily covering about 12,000 miles in your veins, arteries and capillaries, and there are more than 100,000 miles of blood vessels in your body.

The brain, with 100 billion neurons, is the universe's most intricate computer. It's what all computers are modeled after. Your brain can store the same amount of information as 20,000 dictionaries. There are so many nerve cells in the brain—roughly 86 billion—that it would take almost three years to count them. Each neuron can transmit 1,000 nerve impulses per second and make as many as tens of thousands of synaptic contacts with other neurons. A piece of brain tissue the size of a grain of sand contains 100,000 neurons and 1 billion synapses, all communicating with each other. There are as many as 10,000 specific types of neurons in the brain. Humans don't have the largest brains in the world yet the human brain, weighing only about three pounds in adults, gives us the ability to reason and think on our feet beyond the capabilities of the rest of the animal kingdom. Brain information travels up to 268 miles per hour. And as any parent can attest, teenage brains are not fully formed. It isn't until the age of 25 that the human brain reaches full maturity with all the important connections in place.

Our bodies have impressive healing skills in a variety of ways. Bones can heal themselves; skin—the largest organ of the body—constantly replaces itself. The brain can make new connections thanks to neuroplasticity; lungs can generate healthy cells when someone quits smoking. But the liver has truly incredible self-repair capabilities. It can regenerate up to 70% of itself if injured. Although we have 2 kidneys, only one is needed to survive.

A baby is born with over 300 bones, which reduces to 206 for adults as some of the bones fuse together. Bones are four times stronger than concrete and more than half of the bones in the human body are found in the hands and feet.

Human eyes can differentiate between more than ten million colors. The nose can recognize and remember 50,000 different scents, and humans sneeze at speeds of up to 100 mph! Human skin has thousands of sensors that detect sensation and relay information to the brain. All these statistics show that the human body is quite rightly regarded as a miracle. Lastly, do you think you are in control of your life? Don't be so sure. 95% of your decisions take place in your subconscious mind!

So why go to all the trouble of telling you how great the human brain and body are? I'm hoping that by learning how amazing and wonderful they are, you will enjoy and take good care of your miraculous brain and body for many years to come. They are truly a gift. And so are you!

APPENDIX A

Resources

The **Key Questions** this book seeks to answer are: "How do we eliminate the pain of depression and the uncertainty of anxiety? How can we shift from dread and despair to a consciousness of inner peace, tranquility and hope for a better, brighter, more fulfilling future? Here are some helpful tips and suggestions, some of which can benefit you immediately:

1. Seek professional counseling

Call the National Suicide Prevention Lifeline, a United States-based suicide prevention network of over 160 crisis centers that provides 24/7 service via a toll-free hotline with the number

1-800-273-8255 (TALK). It is available to anyone in suicidal crisis or emotional distress. The caller is routed to the nearest crisis center to receive immediate counseling and local mental health referrals. Another quick way to get help is simply dial 988. A live person will answer and refer you to a licensed professional.

2. Talk to someone you trust, who might be a friend, family member, or if it feels appropriate, contact a professional, licensed therapist at the number above.

Other helpful options:

3. The Healing Power of Writing: Great teachers, gurus and mentors have been praising the benefits of personal writing—also called journaling—for hundreds of years. An important technique to shift out of *the suicide room* is to write in a journal every day. Get a spiral notebook and simply write down what you're feeling, what's been happening and any other topics that come to mind—and don't worry about spelling or punctuation. No one is going to read it except you unless you decide to share it with a friend, family member or a counselor. You'll find that when you pursue this process of journaling and "get it off your chest," it helps. You take all that depression, stress and anxiety out of your head and put it into your notebook. Hundreds of thousands of people, suffering from depression, rage, anger, guilt—and a host of other emotions—have used this technique to shift out of the suicide room and into the room of creative expression. Some have written songs, or created art projects or turned their life stories into books, plays or movies. Creative expression—in whatever form you choose—has been a lifesaver for many people, turning them away from self-destruction to more creative ways of dealing with life's challenges. This includes writing, art, music, dance, sculpture, cooking, gardening, poetry, acting and many other ways to express oneself to overcome the pain and stress of daily living.

NOTE: There are many books you can get on journaling, but the one I recommend, which has helped me, is, *The Artist's Way*, by Julia Cameron. Explore the unique personal power of writing, whether it is simply a private daily journal entry of your current personal journey, or even writing your own life story.

When I returned from Vietnam, I decided to become a writer, but that career was derailed when I accepted the high school teaching position. Years later, however, I attended Screenwriting School in Hollywood and eventually wrote a screenplay for a movie. I also began a novel with a goal of writing one page per day. That novel had many interruptions because we moved ten times in six years (lots of different rooms!). It took twenty-five years to complete.

The main premise of my novel is that the soul who was Jesus is asked to return to earth to clear up all the confusion about the many Christian religions. Sound familiar?

After finally completing that novel, I attended a writing workshop at our local library and got an idea for another novel. My second novel was completed in less than two years. It is called *The Chameleon*, about a young man who grows up with both human and other types of blood flowing through his veins due to some experiments his parents, both scientists, were involved in to create cures and vaccines to heal major illnesses.

After completing *The Chameleon*, I began a sequel. Along the way, about 75 pages into it, I got a strong nudge to write a book about my year in Vietnam. The recurring "nudge" became so powerful an impulse that I had to set aside my sequel and begin *Suicide Survivor*. Blocking my efforts, however, was some approach-avoidance about it. Why? Because many parts of my life would be revealed, some that I regretted or wasn't proud of. However, I decided that if my book could help even one person change their mind, go into a different room—change their state of consciousness—and avoid suicide, then it would be worth it. All of these "rooms" were fabulous additions to my life that I never would have discovered had I pulled the trigger years earlier in Vietnam in 1967.

4. Develop a Social Network. Interact with people. What are your hobbies or interests? Many depressed people are lonely and isolated. They have no one to talk with and not enough to do with their time. There are a large variety of special interest groups you might consider. Check with your local library, senior center, or Chamber of Commerce. Ask them what activities they have. Yes, alone time is important and necessary, but so is social interaction for ideal mental health.

5. Get more involved in life. Take up a hobby; learn a language or how to play a musical instrument. Start watching TED Talks, which are only fifteen minutes long but have some incredibly powerful stories. There is a whole world of information and entertainment out there if you simply turn your attention away from yourself—which can seem cramped, isolated and stifling—and instead out into the world, where "cooperators are standing by" to assist your personal journey into a vital, productive and healthy lifestyle.

6. Forgive Yourself. Everyone makes mistakes. We all "fall off the horse," to use a cliché, but you have to get back on the horse as soon as possible. There is another saying, which provides good advice: "Quitters never win and winners never quit." So if you want to win this game called life, then you have to keep going. Try new things. Take up a hobby. Get new friends. Go back to school. Get another job. End toxic relationships, including relationships with anything that negatively affects your health, and be open to new and better ones. Learn from your mistakes and do better next time. Make this your motto: "Every day in every way, I'm getting better and better!" For every question in life there is always an answer. And for every problem you may be facing, there is always a solution. Be persistent until you find the solutions and answers you need. Make it an adventure!

APPENDIX B

Ending Your Life Is Not the Answer to Your Situation

This article by Stan Popovich for the Village News in Fallbrook, CA, has some good advice. He writes: You are at the end of your rope and you can't take it any longer. You are in pain and you are suffering and you feel there is no hope. The first step you need to do is to seek professional help. Do not make the decision to end your life when you are in these kinds of fearful situations.

Here are six reasons why **suicide** and fear are not options regarding your problems.

1. Things change over time. Regardless of your situation, things do not stay the same. You may feel very bad today, but it won't last forever. Everything changes over time. This includes your current situation.

2. There are always other options. You may feel lost and confused, but the answers to your specific problems are out there. The key is that you have to find the answers; the answers to your problems will not come to you. As mentioned before, the first step in finding the solution to your problem is to seek help from a qualified professional.

3. You can't predict the future. Remember that no one can predict the future with 100 percent certainty. Even if the thing that you are afraid of does happen, there are circumstances and factors that you can't predict which can be used to your advantage. For instance, let's say at your place of work that you miss the deadline for a project you have been working on for the last few months. Everything you feared is coming true. Suddenly, your boss comes to your office and tells you that the deadline is extended and that he forgot to tell you the day before. This unknown factor changes everything.

4. Focus on the facts of your situation and not your thoughts. When people are depressed, they rely on their fearful, depressing, and negative thoughts. Your fearful thoughts are exaggerated and are not based on reality. When you are depressed, focus on the facts of your current situation and not on what you think. Do not assume anything regarding your current situation.

5. Go to the hospital when it is that bad. If things are so bad that you are unable to function, drop everything and go to your local hospital or crisis center immediately. The people at the hospital will take care of your situation right away.

6. No situation is hopeless. There are many people and organizations that are willing to help you, but you must be willing to take advantage of this help. Regardless of your situation, take advantage of the assistance that is around you. Every problem has a solution. You just have to find it.

APPENDIX C

Why to Stay

Dese'Rae L. Stage keeps a list of things that make her happy. She learned a long time ago that gratifying distractions and reminders of life's small pleasures might save her in a moment of crisis. She knows this from personal experience, and is the creator of *Live Through This*, a group that documents the portraits and stories of suicide attempt survivors. She's learned that attempting suicide is not a death sentence. Indeed, 9 out of 10 people who attempt to take their own lives and survive do not eventually die by suicide, according to research cited by Harvard's School of Public Health. Avoiding, evading or handling suicidal thoughts can get easier over time, especially once you develop a set of skills to deal with negative or volatile emotions. A key element to success is to create a support network of friends, family, a therapist and a support group.

Below are some examples of why people stayed after attempting suicide:

"I stay because I discovered I'm not ready to go." Lex Tobin

"I stay because living and loving are not possible if I am gone. I would miss all of this senseless beauty. Making the world a better place for my granddaughters is worth any pain." Cheryl Sharp

---

"I stay because I'm now in a unique position to educate, advocate, offer hope and save lives." LIZ MITCHELL

"A dear friend's brother died by suicide several years ago. The memory of his funeral—of the intense singular suffering that comes with losing a loved one to suicide—has kept me from ever attempting suicide again. No matter how bad my depression gets, I know that there are people who would be devastated if they lost me. And when it's too hard for me to live for myself, when every cell in my body wants to give up, I tell myself that I will keep living for them, and I do." MELODY MOEZZI

"My purpose in life is to educate people on suicide via a lived experience perspective. That keeps me going if I have bad days." CAITLIN COLEMAN

"I stay for my dog. I stay for my family. I stay to see what I'll create next." LOGAN

"I stay because my students deserve an adult who always puts them first and fights for their well-being." MARIE

"I stay because if I leave, what is my story going to tell? I want those people who are feeling the way I have felt to know that things can get better. To know it's OK to ask for help even if it seems stupid. To realize that maybe one day you'll find what you are looking for, but even if you don't, things will be OK. I want to have a story. Not one cut short by frustration." CAYLA

"I STAY BECAUSE THERE ARE SO MANY MORE ADVENTURES TO BE HAD AND SO MANY FIRES OF HOPE IN PEOPLE'S SOULS TO IGNITE." Rihanna Brank

---

"I don't have one big reason. Instead, I have thousands of little reasons, ranging from family and friends to the episodes of Bob's Burgers that I won't get to see. Each reason, no matter how small, is an act of resistance that my suicidal thoughts would have to mow down." Alyse Ruriani

---

"I stay because I finally found long-term happiness. While it was terrifying to realize that I now had to relearn how to function as a happy person, it was worth it all. I stay because I want people to know of all the things I live with and have lived through, and to see that I am not only still here, but I am truly happy." CECILIA MARKOW

"I was given a second chance at life, so I stay because 1) I want to honor the people who saved my life and 2) I'm stubborn." Tina Aspegren

---

"I stay because life is full of beautiful surprises that I can't even fathom yet. I think of all I would've missed out on if my attempt had been successful. The most important: I never would've been an aunt and watched my nieces grow. I stay so they will have me to support them." MELANIE DEMOREE

"I choose to stay for my two cats, the people I love and hold dear, the next gorgeous sunrise and epic thunderstorm, and the next good book or awesome cup of tea. The biggest reason I choose to stay is because I'm not ready to choose to go." Ashley Shoemaker

---

"I'M NOT WHO I THOUGHT I WAS. I WANT TO STICK AROUND AND FIND OUT WHO I BECOME." Paul Currington

---

Personally, I stayed because the last-minute timing was too miraculous. I immediately understood that it simply wasn't my time to go. There was too much "divine intervention" occurring that I couldn't ignore. Deep down, I really didn't want to die. And when my suicide attempt was interrupted, it was no longer something I had to do. I let go of any connection I had to Jesus or Judas in past lives. The reasoning on which I had based my former conclusions came crashing down like a house of cards. I was free to live!

The Author

---

* Portions of this chapter from Reader's Digest Dec 23/Jan 24, and attributed to Mashable 2023 by Mashable, Inc., A Ziff Davis Company

As for thoughts of suicide and the pain brought on by depression, the answer is that there are many ways to deal with the pain if you are willing to look for them—and most importantly—to ask for help. It is my fondest wish that this book helps you find some answers—your answers—that will get you back on track to enjoy the best that life has to offer! Always remember: God is *incomplete* without you! And there's a lot you still don't know about the rest of your life! Your challenge is to stay around long enough to find out what it is!

Not the End!

Acknowledgements

This was in many ways a difficult book to write. I had to unpack thoughts and feelings I hadn't looked at for over 50 years. Once I got them out and dusted them off, however, there was still ongoing anxiety and avoidance, which continued to slow the process. The overriding motivation, though, was that my story might help at least one person avoid suicide. I want to thank my friends at the Hilltop Center for Spiritual Living, several of whom read the manuscript. Mark Born, Si Osgrove. Lorraine Buell and my brother, Bob Baker, also read the book early on, offering many helpful suggestions. Hajime Ono, an artist at the Fallbrook Art Association, agreed to do the cover design, sharing with me that he had lost several family members to suicide. Big thanks to Joel Pitney of launchmybook.com, who suggested a major restructuring of the book, which moved everything into the right place. Lastly, a loving thanks to my wife, Karen, who combines the roles of cheerleader, editor, and critic—and always with my best interest at heart!

Note: Seven years after leaving Vietnam, I bumped into Sean Murphy at a Spiritual Conference on Past Lives, Dreams and Freedom from Rebirth. We had each found the same spiritual teaching and have remained friends ever since.

Razors pain you;
Rivers are damp;
Acids stain you;
And drugs cause cramp.
Guns aren't lawful;
Nooses give;
Gas smells awful;
You might as well live.

Dorothy Parker

"Underrated life advice: You can reinvent yourself as many times as you need. New habits. New standards. New people. New career. You're never stuck. You're allowed to change. Today, tomorrow, and as many times as it takes to create the life you want."

—Sahil Bloom

www.ingramcontent.com/pod-product-compliance
Lightning Source LLC
LaVergne TN
LVHW100327210926
848480LV00003B/1278
9798999600004